DR. SINGH'S SCHOOL OF CHILDREN

MINDSET IS A SUPERPOWER!

THE SUPERPOWER OF RESILIENCE

DR. SINGH'S SCHOOL OF CHILDREN

MINDSET IS A *SUPERPOWER!*

THE SUPERPOWER OF RESILIENCE

BINAY SINGH

TWAGAA

HTTPS://TWAGAA.COM

TWAGAA
HTTPS://TWAGAA.COM

Mumbai (MH), India
Website: https://twagaa.com
Email: hello@twagaa.com

First published by TWAGAA INTERNATIONAL 2020

Title: Dr. Singh's School of Children : Mindset is a Superpower! : The Superpower of Resilience

ISBN: 978-93-91254-52-0

First Edition
Printed in India

Ordering Information:
Quantity sales: Special discounts are available on quantity purchases by corporations, associations, and others. For details, contact the publisher at the address or email above.

ACKNOWLEDGEMENTS

I am so blessed by our great Almighty that he gave me the blessing of always loving to be with our children. I visited an orphanage - "Ribnikov's Children Orphanage" - with my bosom friend Misha, my recent good friend Anton Korynevych, Representative of the Ukrainian President for the Crimean region, and one of my best friends, Timur Korotkiy.

After meeting eight cute boys and a beautiful girl, I was very much inspired to write a book to help with their positivity and bright careers. I believe if I write books on Children's Soft Skills, they will be very helpful for children across the globe.

I am very grateful to my mother for her kind blessing to write this series of books, "Dr. Singh's School of Children". And I am very thankful to my family and my son for their kind support to write this series of books.

I am more than grateful to my friend Timur Korotkiy for his awesome and inspiring Foreword.

Also, my sincere thanks to my friend Amy for her kind help in structuring this book properly.

Thanks to everyone in this world for their kind blessing and support.

CONTENTS

INTRODUCTION

For children, it is necessary to learn to be resilient.

There are two main reasons behind this. Resilience helps children face small challenges that arise in their day-to-day life, such as minor obstacles or disappointments in school or at home. It has also proved to be beneficial in helping children through major hardships, such as bullying and mental health struggles.

Children are often prone to suffering significant stress under such circumstances because they don't have the necessary coping mechanisms to seek the help they need or accurately express how they are feeling. However, when children are resilient they can endure the stress caused by these events. This also changes how they look back on these negative events.

They often can use the experience to learn and grow, whereas children who may not have resilience may find these negative experiences more traumatic. There are many ways to go about building resilience in children, but one of the most entertaining ways is by using games. It helps encourage the child to work through the challenging parts of a game, ask for help when needed and support their peers to ensure that the game is played by them as well.

Read this book to know more about how kids can be more resilient.

Let's dive in.

WHY KIDS NEED TO LEARN RESILIENCE

We've all been there: our kids are complaining about something and we catch ourselves saying things like "when I was a kid" or "back in my day". It slips out without us even thinking about it!

While it's tempting to think that kids these days have it easy, the reality is that the pressures on them are greater than ever. There's far more academic stress and it starts at an earlier age. Plus, social media has fundamentally changed the way we communicate and engage with others, which can have a major effect on our children's mental health. We see this in the levels of anxiety and other mental health conditions among children: One in four adolescents and one in seven primary school kids experience mental health problems.
It's easy to think that this is all very doom-and-gloom- that there's nothing positive to be gained from this. In fact, the opposite is the case. The fact that we understand so much about the pressures on young people today means that we can work to teach them skills that will help them in the challenges they're facing.

What's the most important of these skills?
It's resilience.

That response might raise more questions than answers,

so let's dive into what we mean by resilience. What is it? Simply put, resilience is the capacity to respond to stress or adversity positively. You might think of it as the ability to withstand pressure without crumbling.

SO, WHY DO KIDS NEED TO LEARN RESILIENCE?

Norman Garmezy, a developmental psychologist, has researched resilience in children and found a remarkable trend. His research demonstrates that children can flourish even in the face of serious trials if they are resilient. Rather than only considering how to alleviate the negative impact of stress, Gamezy's research shows that resilience can help protect children from the negative impact of stress, and prevent long-lasting after-effects of difficult situations.

There are two kinds of adversity that psychologists have identified for young people: first, low-level adversity, and second, major adversity.

Low-level adversity is the sort of pressure that's present in everyday life. While your kids might think you asking them to tidy their room or do their homework is adversity, what we mean is the general stress that comes from things like school pressure or challenges in social scenarios.

Major adversity looks a little different. It's a more severe type of stress that comes as a result of bigger problems. This can be things like learning disabilities impacting schoolwork, or mental health issues. It can even be things like bullying or grief.

Whether it's low-level or major adversity, it's clear that children experience pressures and stresses just as adults do. The impact of this kind of stress only increases with age. As much as we might joke with our kids about how hard we had it as youngsters, the fact of the matter is that 65% of adolescents nowadays won't seek help for their mental health issues. Early intervention is key.

How can you tell if your child has resilience already? Emmy Werner, another developmental psychologist, has found that people with resilience generally have shared indicators of how they grew that resilience. There are several settings in which resilience is developed. Sometimes, it's a result of our environment; strong relationships with caregivers, parents, teachers, or mentors have a big impact. However, it's also important to know that resilient children have what Werner terms an internal locus of control. They see themselves as controlling their own destiny.

Sure, a lot of our kids think they're in control. Battling with a toddler over bedtime will definitely convince you that they think they're in control! However, in this scenario, Werner's research refers more to the idea of perception. Children with resilience perceive themselves as capable of responding to stressors, and seeing them as an opportunity for new knowledge. They don't necessarily perceive stressful events as traumatic and therefore don't experience them as traumatic.

So, you might think your child is naturally quite resilient. It's true that some people simply are more resilient than others! Fortunately, however, it's not true that resilience is only something we're born with—we can absolutely learn it, too.

Resilience can be learned in several settings, which means that teaching your kids to be resilient can be something personalized to who they are as people. It's something that can be learned at school or at home, or with the help of a professional like a therapist, counselor, or psychologist.

Schools are coming to understand more and more the importance of childhood mental health and the impact that resilience can have. As academic pressure begins at a younger age than ever, it's so important for schools to recognize the effects this can have on children's mental health. By building in programs and activities that foster good mental health, schools can build resilience in their pupils.

Parents are also key to building resilience in kids. Changing the family's attitude to schoolwork, for example, valuing the process of learning over only achieving high grades helps teach kids a growth mindset—a key part of resilience. Choosing to reframe negative events into learning opportunities has a similar impact. Similarly, engaging with your kids to be grateful and mindful, and to let go of negative thoughts, means that you're building their resilience. Don't worry, though—if the prospect of meditating with your kids fills you with fear, there are a lot of ways to achieve mindfulness!

Overall, it's clear that resilience helps kids tackle life challenges and reduces the impact that stress has on them. From the low-level adversity of everyday life to the major adversity of life-changing situations, resilience is a tool that will help your child to both survive and thrive. From resilience-building activities at school to practicing gratitude at home, there are plenty of ways for you to teach your kids resilience in a manner that suits you.

A RESILIENCE GUIDE FOR PARENTS AND TEACHERS

While it's tempting to think otherwise, childhood pressure is greater than ever. Everything from everyday anxieties about schoolwork to major life events like grief or learning difficulties, the pressure on our kids is greater than it's ever been. This has a major impact on children's mental health and can have long-lasting effects into adulthood.

Resilience is a skill that's invaluable in tackling this kind of pressure. It acts as a lifejacket—instead of tackling the negative after-effects of pressure, resilience protects children from suffering those after-effects. Fortunately, resilience is a skill that not only has a long-lasting and positive effect, but is also something that improves mental health.

So, here are 8 great ways for you to teach resilience to your kids or students!

☛ CREATE DAILY ROUTINES

Parents and teachers alike can attest that kids thrive with routine. After all, we all know the impact of messing with things like bedtime! When you work with your kids to determine a daily routine, you allow them to feel like they have some control, whilst also giving them the support of a routine and boundaries. Make sure there are times for work and play.

Naturally, there's always going to be times when you need to be flexible in your routine—holidays, for example, or unexpected events. That's ok! By including kids in developing the daily routine and communicating the process to them, you're preparing them to ride out changes to that daily routine. That's resilience in action!

☛ TAKE REGULAR BREAKS

While it's important to allow your kids the opportunity to meet challenges and to try new things, it's also valuable to allow them the space to take a break from doing so. Allow them to talk over their concerns and fears, or to focus on the things that they can control. You're building resilience by showing them how to validate and understand all their feelings, not just positive ones.

☛ BUILD RELATIONSHIPS

As tempting as it is to think that our kids are entirely focused on themselves, the reality is that they thrive when they're building relationships with other people and engaging with their peers. Not only is this a vital social experience, but it also offers opportunities for kids to see examples of resilience and to learn how to see the world from different perspectives. Both of these are vital kinds of knowledge that will help them to foster resilience.

At home, encourage your kids to build and maintain relationships with others. This can be through things like joining clubs or sports teams, inviting friends over, or even just speaking on the phone. Alternatively, it could be something like starting up a pen-pal correspondence with an older family member, like a grandparent. In the classroom, encourage group projects as well as individual work to strengthen peer-to-peer social support.

☛ DO ACTS OF SERVICE

This ties into number 3! Kids get the opportunity to see just how capable they are when they're helping other people. If you think it'd be a useful way for your child to build their resilience, try enrolling them in age-appropriate volunteering, or getting them to help the rest of the family with jobs and tasks. For teachers, try chatting with your students about how they can help each other in the classroom.

☛ COMMIT TO SELF-CARE

Teaching kids self-care is invaluable when it comes to building resilience. This can be things like eating well, getting enough sleep, or doing exercise or activities. However, it can also be things like developing a positive view of themselves by remembering the successes they've had in the past and the lessons they've learned. For example, as a parent you might encourage your kids to remember how they tried a new activity that they were nervous about; as a teacher, you can talk about how they're a valuable member of the classroom.

SET GOALS

Setting goals to work towards is a fantastic way for kids to develop resilience. It nurtures their sense of personal responsibility. Moreover, it gives kids a sense of purpose to work towards a goal in small increments. At school, this might look something like breaking up tasks into smaller pieces; at home, perhaps it's regularly practicing things like musical instruments or sports. By having the end goal in sight but developing a plan as to how to get there, you're teaching your kids the skills of resilience to keep pushing on.

This is a great way of building resilience because it also encourages kids to see the bigger picture and keep a hold of their perspective. We've all seen our kids have meltdowns over things that we think are inconsequential! By teaching them to keep an eye on the big picture, you encourage them to keep going when things go wrong by pointing to the progress they've made so far.

☛ LOOK FOR LEARNING

Difficult moments are often the best teachers. When things are tough, encourage children to look at the situation as a learning opportunity, and ask them how they might respond to the challenge. In a school environment, you can also nurture this kind of resilience by leading discussions about learning opportunities students have had in the past. This helps to develop what we might term a growth mindset; kids learn how to see mistakes, failures, or disappointments as chances to grow.

☛ ACCEPT CHANGE

Change can be a frightening prospect for anyone, especially for children and young people. To tackle this fear, teach kids to see change as a normal part of life. It's helpful to show them that change can be a good thing, and can be an opportunity for growth. By embracing change, kids learn to be adaptable and resilient.

Overall, kids thrive in environments that allow them the chance to build their resilience. From working with their peers to serving others, and from learning about self-care to accepting change, these examples are a great place to start.

GAMES & ACTIVITIES FOR KIDS & PARENTS TO BUILD RESILIENCE

GAMES WITH PEERS VS. SOLO GAMES

When playing games with others they recognize that they can ask for support when they need it. They are able to experience an event that may create stress, but they are not alone and they have their peers to seek help from when they need to. It provides the child with a sense of security and acceptance. When doing things solo they are understanding and validating their experience, and with the help of an adult they can reframe their negative memories in a more positive manner. Both types of games are equally effective; they just require different amounts of effort from the child.

RESILIENCE GAMES

☛ HULA-HOOP GAME

The hula-hoop game is challenging, but helps children build resilience by having them develop a solution to a problem in that moment. Although there are numerous activities that require children to come up with a creative solution when facing a challenge, this activity is unique because it encourages everyone playing to work together to find a creative solution to help them progress towards their collective goal: getting the hula-hoop around the circle.

How to play:

- Have students stand in a circle

- Children should hold the hand of each person standing next to them
- Before the last hand holding connection, place hula-hoop on one students arm
- Have students move hula-hoop around the circle until it comes back to whoever started without letting go of each other's hand

This can be a difficult game because children have to find a way to fit through the hula-hoop in order to pass it along to the person next to them. Students will also have to support the student passing the hula-hoop so that they don't fall over. However, it encourages them to use their creative thinking, feedback from peers and allows them to celebrate after overcoming the challenge.

LOVE LETTER TO A CLASSMATE

This activity helps children learn about the importance of kindness for others as well as themselves. This activity requires each student to be given one of their peers' names. Whoever's name they get is who they write a love letter to. Inside the love letter they can include drawings and things they love and admire about their classmate. You can also allow the children to use fun paper, markers, paint, and glitter. This allows them to visually express how they feel while also expressing love and gratitude verbally to their peers. When they are done with their love letter they can go and give it to whoever their love letter is for. After receiving their letter, have the children draw or write about how they felt about giving and receiving their love letter.

☛ UNDERSTANDING THROUGH COLORING

This activity is great for allowing students to explore their feelings and visually express it through color. For this exercise ask the child to recall a memory from their past. It can be happy, sad or exciting. Once they have decided on a memory, ask them to close their eyes and focus on how they felt in that moment. With their eyes still closed place a coloring sheet of a mandala and coloring utensils in front of them. When they open their eyes, have them color in the mandala using colors and materials that represent the emotions they were feeling. After they finish coloring the mandala, ask them to reflect on why they chose the colors.

☛ COMPLIMENT CIRCLE

Practicing kindness plays an important role in the development of resilience in children. This helps boost the self-esteem of the child receiving the compliment while simultaneously encouraging the person giving the compliment to focus on the positives of an individual/ situation.

How to Play:

- Have the kids sit in a circle with their legs extended
- Pick one child to give a compliment first. They will pick another person in the group and give them a compliment of their choosing. For example, a child could compliment their peer by saying, "I like how you always hold the door for me when I'm coming into the building." They should refrain from using compliments that are based on physical traits.
- After a child receives a compliment they bring their legs in and compliment someone else who hasn't yet received one. Continue until everyone in the circle has gotten a compliment.

After completing this exercise, have the children reflect on howpraising and being praised by their peers felt.

☛ TRUST WALK

A trust walk is a great activity to show children to trust their peers. This activity requires the class to be split in half, one half of the class is assigned to be a leader. The leaders are then partnered up with a classmate from the other group. Their partner must wear a blindfold. Whoever is leading must offer clues and bring their peer safely to the end of the obstacle course. This activity places a lot of responsibility on the student directing their classmate because they have to make sure their partner can understand and accurately follow the directions being provided. The children blindfolded must place complete trust in their leader to get them through the obstacle course successfully.

How to Play:

- Divide the class in half, assigning half to be a leader and the other half to be the partner
- Provide the partner with a blindfold (make sure the blindfold completely covers their eyes)
- Have both students hold hands or latch arms
- Have the leader guide their partner through the obstacle course while offering clues
- Once they successfully make their way through the course, have the partners switch so that the leader now becomes the partner

After completing the activity ask them how they felt while completing the obstacle course and whether they liked leading or following more, and why.

☛ RECOGNIZING TRAITS AND TALENTS

This activity encourages students to see their talents, strengths and positive traits as a gift. Thinking of these traits as a gift makes the game more exciting while also allowing a gift box to be created in the end. Children will need a gift box worksheet, scissors, marker, glue and any other craft materials they may want.

To start the exercise, have children focus on who they are on the inside, who they see themselves to be. This first step allows students to identify what gifts and special traits they believe they have. Qualities can include being considerate, kind, patient, mature, outgoing, adventurous, etc.. After the children make their list, have them share it with their peers and explain why they chose the qualities they did. They can also share examples of why they think these traits fit them. Once everyone has shared, children can be provided a box, which they can decorate however they would like. Children can then cut up the words they feel are representative of themselves and place them in the box. This is a great activity because it allows children to really examine who they are and what positive traits they possess.

DEVELOPING THE PREFRONTAL CORTEX

The prefrontal cortex is the part of the brain responsible for setting goals, focusing attention as well as managing behavior and emotional reactions. Developing and strengthening the prefrontal cortex helps increase a child's capacity to develop coping mechanisms. The prefrontal cortex plays a big role in the character development of a child and helps them make conscious decisions that support their motivations.

Ways to help develop Prefrontal Cortex:

- Setting routines
- Encouraging activities and games that encourage creativity, such as painting, drawing, playing pretend
- Board games
- Encourage children to be patient while they wait for their turn, plan ahead for their next move and improve memory functions
- Encouraging and modeling healthy social behaviour
- Providing the child the option and environment to make new friends and encouraging them to maintain these relationships they create
- Exercise
- Encouraging children to make their own decisions
- Encouraging children to be more independent in their day to day life

HOW PARENTS CAN HELP

Parents play an essential role in helping children become more resilient. They can help provide children the building blocks that encourage resilience and perseverance. A few ways in which parents can help are:

☛ ***Help practice mindfulness***

Parents can help their children practice mindfulness by providing them journal prompts that encourage them to think about the way they feel and why they might be feeling that way. These journal prompts can explore emotions, passions and activities they did that day. This is a great way for children to reflect on any mistakes they may have made and learn from them. It also allows children the opportunity to share any exciting or positive moments from their day.

☛ ***Exercise***

Ensuring that children have some sort of physical activity is greatly beneficial to their overall development. Exercise helps strengthen the brain and make it more resilient to stress. There are many fun activities you can do with your child, such as:

- Throwing a frisbee
- Going on a walk
- Bike ride
- Dance

☛ ***Practice gratitude***

Having children practice gratitude during the day is a

fantastic tool to help them through challenges and stress later on. When you encourage your child to practice gratitude it encourages them to look for the positives in situations before looking for the negative. By doing so they can view their most challenging experiences as a learning experience rather than looking back on them as a traumatic memory. Parents can encourage gratitude practices by having a child list ten good things that happened during the day or asking them to list off ten things they love and appreciate about themselves or the people around them.

☛ ***Teach them how to ask for help and that it's okay to ask for help***

Teaching children how to ask for help and that it's okay to ask for help is an essential skill to learn. It helps the child realize that they do not need to face challenges by themselves, they can seek support and that it will often make challenging times much more bearable. It also allows students to recognize that they shouldn't feel ashamed of seeking help when they need it. Asking for help is a very strong thing to do because it means the child recognizes that they need the help of another individual, which is a very brave thing to do. For example, when you see a child getting frustrated after spending quite a bit of time trying to complete a task, remind them that they can ask for help and that you would be more than willing to support them and help them complete the task at hand.

☛ ***Teach them to face fear, with support***

Children have many fears, often because there is still so much unknown to them. By understanding the things that create a sense of anxiety or fear for your child, you can help them face these obstacles in a constructive way that may help them overcome their fears. Allowing children to face their fears can be extremely empowering and will encourage them to face fears as something that they can gradually approach. Neither does it have to be complete avoidance of a situation nor do they have to throw themselves headfirst into the task at hand.

☛ ***Reframe negative events***

Encouraging children to reframe negative events is essential in order for them to truly utilize a negative experience as a positive learning experience. This encourages children to look for positives within a situation rather than dwelling on the negative. For example, if a child has a playdate scheduled at the playground but for whatever reason the playdate gets cancelled, you can use this opportunity to reframe it from a negative experience into a positive one.

Start by recognizing that your child is upset by the news that they will not be able to play with their friend. Then remind them that they will have many more opportunities to see their friend. Once the child recognizes that they can see their friend on another occasion, start suggesting other fun activities you could do instead to fill the time.

Maybe, you can make cookies or go on a walk through a trail in town. Maybe you could go and visit a museum or the library. Going forward, this allows children to recognize that it is okay to be upset when an event does not go the way it was planned because it can be an opportunity to do something else new and exciting.

Children need to be resilient in the face of adversity in order to get through challenging times throughout their lives. Their ability to work through obstacles later in life can depend on how resilient they were growing up and whether or not their resiliency was nurtured. As a child is growing up, it is important for them to have the building blocks and a strong foundation in place so that when challenges arise later on they do not feel completely helpless.

Resiliency provides a lengthy list of healthy ways to cope with challenging situations. When teaching it to children it is important to encourage it through action first and then follow with a reflection. This is an easy way for children to understand that they have control over their lives and the way they perceive both positive and negative situations. Allowing a child the opportunity to make mistakes, fail and work through challenges allows them the opportunity to learn from them and use what they learn later on in life. When children are encouraged to use failure as something they can learn from rather than something they need to fear, in the future it helps them explore new opportunities.

BUILDING RESILIENCE IN CHILDREN: 20 PRACTICAL, POWERFUL EXERCISES

☛ RESILIENCE AND STRESS: HOW IT WORKS

I'm sure you've heard of the "fight or flight" response. It's the response everyone has when they're faced with something dangerous, overwhelming, challenging or traumatizing. It's when your body goes into overdrive to keep you safe or beefs up your abilities so you can get through something you otherwise probably wouldn't.

Obviously, that response is a good thing, but only when it's for a limited time. When we're in "fight or flight" mode for long periods of time, it causes a lot of mental, physical, and emotional problems that can cause us to break down, give up, or even have serious health issues.

☛ RESILIENCE HELPS KEEP ALL THAT FROM HAPPENING.

See, the "fight or flight" response is made by the amygdala, or the part of our brain that makes us angry, defensive, and ready to act. When the amygdala goes into overdrive, it stops our prefrontal cortex from working, and that's the part of the brain that handles our smart decision making and critical thinking.

Developing resilience trains the prefrontal cortex to kick back in when the amygdala makes it shut off for a bit, and it allows us to start moving past the stress.

☛ EFFECTS OF RESILIENCE ON BEHAVIOR PATTERNS

You can think of resiliency and how it works like a dam. If the dam is small, made of sticks, and poorly built, even a little bit of water can crush it and flood everything on the other side. If it's strong, made of concrete, and built by the best engineers, it can hold back entire rivers.

☛ YOUR RESILIENCY IS THE DAM, AND THE CHALLENGES YOU FACE ARE THE WATER.

How resilient you, or your children, are determines how much you can take before you finally go off the deep end. People with low resilience may have a complete meltdown over their burger not being cooked all the way. Others, with high resiliency, might not feel overwhelmed unless something really traumatic happens and, even then, they tend to bounce back faster than others put in the same situation.

20 RESILIENCE BUILDING STRATEGIES

1. BUILD A SUPPORT SYSTEM

Even the strongest kids can't do it all on their own. They need adults in their lives who fully support them in their struggles, even the silly ones that don't seem like big deals, to help them develop crucial coping skills they can take with them when they're on their own. They don't need tons of supportive adults; even a single pillar of support can completely change their lives.

2. SHOW THEM PEOPLE CARE

This ties in with the first tip. Kids want to know that others care about them. Tell their grandparents, friends, aunts, uncles, teachers, and other people they're close to about all the great things they do, and when those people praise them, let them know. Maybe grandma said, "I am so proud of that boy. He's a brave young man". Tell them about it.

3. ENCOURAGE SEEKING HELP

Yeah, it's a little frustrating to help a kid out non-stop. After all, you can't stop working every five minutes to help with their Lego project or something else. However, it's important to always be supportive and never make them feel ashamed for needing help. Resiliency doesn't always work, and sometimes, they'll need help. If they feel ashamed, they might not ask for help when it's really important.

4. STRENGTHEN THE PREFRONTAL CORTEX

Prefrontal cortex sounds like a fancy word, but it's just the front part of the brain that lets us think critically and make good, well-thought out decisions. Strengthening it can help it overcome the amygdala, or the part that's purely for survival instincts, and lower how much stress a kid has to go through when something bad happens.

5. ENCOURAGE MINDFULNESS

We've written about mindfulness a lot in the past, and it's all about considering everything that is happening in the moment, and how a person's actions affect those around them. Encouraging mindfulness not only strengthens the prefrontal cortex, but it also helps us be better people in general.

6. EXERCISE

Exercise may not seem like it would affect the brain very much, but it does! It relieves stress and helps you vent all your emotions, and it strengthens your body and mind to prevent future stress from affecting it as much. Any fun exercise works for this, too. Whether you want to take your kid out to play frisbee, let them run wild at the park, or have multiple kids play a fast-paced game of tag on the jungle gym, exercise helps build resiliency a lot.

7. BUILD THEIR CONFIDENCE

Confidence is a key part of resiliency. After all, it's what we use when we tell ourselves we can get past an obstacle and succeed, or pick ourselves back up after we fail. Building confidence isn't hard either. Simply challenge your kid to do new things, and praise them when they succeed at something. It'll pay off in the future, and it'll make them feel great in the moment.

8. OPTIMISM OVER PESSIMISM

Having a positive attitude automatically makes someone a lot more likely to bounce back from a big failure or horrible experience, because they'll immediately find the good in the situation. You can help your kid be more optimistic by reframing bad experiences as learning opportunities, always looking on the bright side of life, and letting them know that bad times don't last forever.

9. REFRAME BAD EXPERIENCES AND FAILURES

This ties in with being optimistic. Reframing a failure as a learning experience, or finding something good in a bad situation, helps get rid of some of the stress brought on by those things. For example, if your kid accidentally gets an F on a really easy test because they rushed through and guessed questions they knew the answer to, don't scold them. Let them know that this is a good lesson, that they are more than smart enough to do better, and that they should take their time in the future.

10. BE A ROLE MODEL

Kids don't just want to listen to you preach all day. They want to see you walk the walk and talk the talk. So, do it! Don't just teach them about resiliency, be a resilient person yourself. Don't worry. They're watching your every move.

11. SUPPORT THEM WHEN THEY FACE THEIR FEARS

We all want our kids to face their fears, but oftentimes, we just tell them to do it and leave them all alone. While that helps them be more independent, it doesn't help make them resilient. When your kids are afraid of something, push them to face their fears, but be there to support them while they do it.

12. SUPPORT RISK TAKING; NOT JUST OUTCOMES

Everybody wants to congratulate their kid when they succeed at something, but a lot of us forget to congratulate them just for trying, even when they fail. That's a shame, because it takes a lot of courage to do something that's risky and fail at it. Just make sure they take safe risks. Letting them jump down the stairs and congratulating them probably isn't a great idea.

13. LET THEM HAVE A CHANCE TO SUCCEED

It's tempting to see your kid struggling with a difficult puzzle and immediately rush in to help them, but that's not the way to go. Instead, kids should be allowed to struggle a bit, as long as the situation is safe. If they're having a hard time with their homework, give them a chance to succeed before helping them. If they can't get all the way across the monkey bars on the first try, let them fall a few times and encourage them to keep trying. Of course, if they're struggling too much, a parent's help is always welcome.

14. HELP PROCESS THEIR EMOTIONS

Extreme emotions are hard to handle. Especially negative emotions like shame, embarrassment, or sadness. However, you shouldn't teach your kid to run away from those emotions. Instead, have a one-on-one and help them understand why they're having those feelings, that the feelings are okay, and that it's best to work their way through them in safe, productive ways.

15. ENCOURAGE GROWTH

A growth mindset isn't just something for adults to develop so they can have better lives. They're for kids, too. In fact, helping kids develop growth-based mindsets early on helps them become more resilient, and it helps them get further in life when they're older, without having to go through all the mindset development many adults are just starting to go through.

16. TRUST THEM TO COPE

We've all been there. When our child is suffering, we can't help but want to jump in and make everything better. It's just parental instinct. However, that keeps them from learning to cope on their own. Instead, be supportive, help them when they ask for it, and trust them to cope in their own healthy way without you butting in.

17. TEACH SELF-TALK

Positive self-talk can get people through a lot of hard times, and if you teach it to your kid early, it'll pay off big time later in life, as well as throughout their childhood.

Teach them to tell themselves things such as, “It’s okay. I can do this if I try harder” and “I am good enough to get through this”.

18. ALWAYS PUSH CREATIVITY AND PLAY

You may not think so, but creativity is a huge part of problem solving, and kids learn it from playing. So, letting them play is one of the greatest teaching tools you have at your disposal, and it gives you a break from picking up their messes or worrying about them swinging from the kitchen cabinets.

19. LISTEN

Your kid is going to come to you with every problem they have. Maybe some big bully stole their lunch money, or maybe they don’t understand why the teacher told them to stop jumping on their desk at school. Let them talk about it without flat out answering all their problems. Just guide them towards figuring it out on their own, and they’ll develop a lot of problem solving skills that help build resilience.

20. ASK THEM HOW, NOT WHY

You can ask your kid why they slapped an entire jar of peanut butter between two cold tortillas and chucked their weird concoction at the living room window, but we already know what answer you're going to get: "I don't know". Instead of playing the same back and forth game you always do, ask them how their decision affected them before having them clean it up. If it's something a little more tame like an accident, ask them how they can fix the situation instead of asking them why they did it.

CONCLUSION

Everybody is born with a low amount of resiliency, and external factors, like a loving family, friends, confidence, and everything else, help build resiliency as the child ages.

That's a bad thing if you never put any effort into developing your kid's resiliency, but it's great if you're willing to help. Your potential to help them build resiliency is practically limitless if you're willing to put in the work and deliberately nurture them.

The book delves into various tips, tricks, games, activities and more that can help parents teach resilience to kids.

ABOUT THE AUTHOR

Dr Binay Kumar Singh, Founder & CEO of *Singh Marine Management Ltd.* in Odessa (Ukraine) and Founder & President of *Federation of Global Maritime Community*, is an entrepreneur, author, and public speaker. His life mission is to serve the world's communities and guide everyone through positivity, love, and enthusiasm. This is reflected in his simple and timeless life philosophy: "Treat people as you like to be treated."

Dr Singh has a Master of Science in Marine Navigation and a Doctorate of Philosophy. He is a globally recognized expert in international shipping with over two decades of experience. Dr Singh is also taking wonderful measures for the needy community of the society as well. His new project with the name "Selfless Fund" is specifically targeted to help those who are in need. Dr Singh has also launched his new company GSR which is going to bring innovations to the shipping and maritime industry. His efforts for the shipping industry as well as for the society is an example of his generosity and selflessness.

He enjoys pursuing multiple passions like singing, dancing, playing the piano and the accordion, and keeping healthy by practicing yoga and CrossFit.

Email: binaysingh@gsr.international
Website: https://drbinaysingh.com

MORE BOOKS BY DR BINAY SINGH

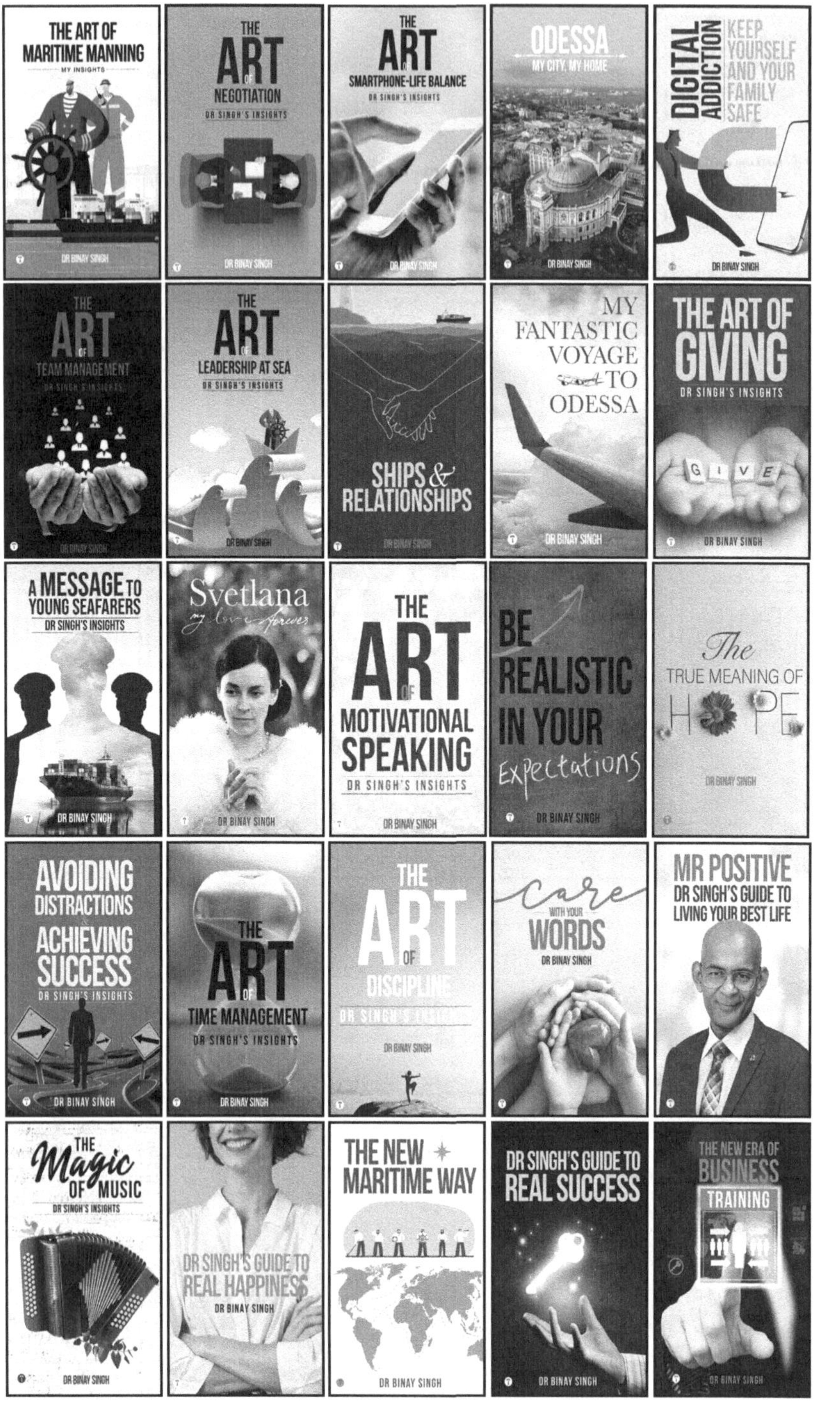
THE ART OF MARITIME MANNING
MY INSIGHTS
DR BINAY SINGH
THE ART OF NEGOTIATION
DR SINGH'S INSIGHTS
DR BINAY SINGH
THE ART OF SMARTPHONE-LIFE BALANCE
DR SINGH'S INSIGHTS
DR BINAY SINGH
ODESSA
MY CITY, MY HOME
DR BINAY SINGH
DIGITAL ADDICTION
KEEP YOURSELF AND YOUR FAMILY SAFE
DR BINAY SINGH
THE ART OF TEAM MANAGEMENT
DR SINGH'S INSIGHTS
DR BINAY SINGH
THE ART OF LEADERSHIP AT SEA
DR SINGH'S INSIGHTS
DR BINAY SINGH
SHIPS & RELATIONSHIPS
DR BINAY SINGH
MY FANTASTIC VOYAGE TO ODESSA
DR BINAY SINGH
THE ART OF GIVING
DR SINGH'S INSIGHTS
GIVE
DR BINAY SINGH
A MESSAGE TO YOUNG SEAFARERS
DR SINGH'S INSIGHTS
DR BINAY SINGH
Svetlana
my love forever
DR BINAY SINGH
THE ART OF MOTIVATIONAL SPEAKING
DR SINGH'S INSIGHTS
DR BINAY SINGH
BE REALISTIC IN YOUR Expectations
DR BINAY SINGH
The TRUE MEANING OF HOPE
DR BINAY SINGH
AVOIDING DISTRACTIONS
ACHIEVING SUCCESS
DR SINGH'S INSIGHTS
DR BINAY SINGH
THE ART OF TIME MANAGEMENT
DR SINGH'S INSIGHTS
DR BINAY SINGH
THE ART OF DISCIPLINE
DR SINGH'S INSIGHTS
DR BINAY SINGH
Care WITH YOUR WORDS
DR BINAY SINGH
MR POSITIVE
DR SINGH'S GUIDE TO LIVING YOUR BEST LIFE
THE Magic OF MUSIC
DR SINGH'S INSIGHTS
DR BINAY SINGH
DR SINGH'S GUIDE TO REAL HAPPINESS
DR BINAY SINGH
THE NEW MARITIME WAY
DR BINAY SINGH
DR SINGH'S GUIDE TO REAL SUCCESS
DR BINAY SINGH
THE NEW ERA OF BUSINESS
TRAINING
DR BINAY SINGH